MOVIE QUARTETS FOR ALL

Playable on ANY FOUR INSTRUMENTS
or any number of instruments in ensemble

Arranged by Michael Story

Alfred

ISBN-10: 0-7390-6327-8
ISBN-13: 978-0-7390-6327-9

HEDWIG'S THEME
(From "Harry Potter and the Sorcerer's Stone" - 2001)

FLUTE/PICCOLO

By **JOHN WILLIAMS**
Arranged by MICHAEL STORY

Mysteriously

*G♭ = F♯

OVER THE RAINBOW
(From "The Wizard of Oz" - 1939)

Music by HAROLD ARLEN
Lyrics by E.Y. HARBURG
Arranged by MICHAEL STORY

AND ALL THAT JAZZ
(From "Chicago" - 2002)

Lyrics by FRED EBB
Music by JOHN KANDER
Arranged by MICHAEL STORY

8

THE MAGNIFICENT SEVEN
(From "The Magnificent Seven" - 1960)

By ELMER BERNSTEIN
Arranged by MICHAEL STORY

THEME FROM "A SUMMER PLACE"
(From "A Summer Place" - 1959)

Words by MACK DISCANT
Music by MAX STEINER
Arranged by MICHAEL STORY

D.C. al Coda

EYE OF THE TIGER
(From "Rocky III" - 1982)

Words and Music by
FRANKIE SULLIVAN III and JIM PETERIK
Arranged by MICHAEL STORY

Moderate rock ♩ = 120

HAKUNA MATATA
(From Walt Disney's "The Lion King" - 1994)

Music by ELTON JOHN
Words by TIM RICE
Arranged by MICHAEL STORY

THERE YOU'LL BE
(From "Pearl Harbor" - 2001)

Words and Music by
DIANE WARREN
Arranged by MICHAEL STORY

BLUES IN THE NIGHT
(From "Blues in the Night" - 1941)

Words by JOHNNY MERCER
Music by HAROLD ARLEN
Arranged by MICHAEL STORY

Moderate blues

THE PINK PANTHER
(From "The Pink Panther" - 1963, 2006)

By HENRY MANCINI
Arranged by MICHAEL STORY

PARADE OF THE CHARIOTEERS
(From "Ben-Hur" - 1959)

By MIKLOS ROZSA
Arranged by MICHAEL STORY

YOU'RE A MEAN ONE, MR. GRINCH
(From "How the Grinch Stole Christmas" - 1966, 2000)

Lyrics by DR. SEUSS
Music by ALBERT HAGUE
Arranged by MICHAEL STORY